Guide to Dart

Practical Guide

V. Telman

Copyright © 2024

Guide to Dart

1.Introduction to Dart

Dart is a versatile, open-source programming language developed by Google. It was designed to be an all-purpose language that excels in various domains, particularly for client-side development. Its primary use case is for building mobile, desktop, server, and web applications. Dart is the language behind Flutter, Google's popular UI toolkit for building natively compiled applications for mobile, web, and desktop from a single codebase.

History and Evolution

Dart was first announced by Google at the GOTO conference in October 2011. The initial aim was to replace JavaScript as the main language for web development due to perceived limitations in JavaScript's performance and scalability. However, over time, Dart evolved into a more versatile language. The first stable version of Dart was released in November 2013, and since then, it has undergone significant changes and improvements. One of the most notable milestones in Dart's history was the introduction of Flutter in 2017, which significantly boosted Dart's popularity.

Features of Dart

Dart is a robust language equipped with a variety of features that make it a powerful tool for developers. Here are some of the key features:

1. **Compiled and Interpreted**: Dart can be both compiled to native code and interpreted. This dual capability allows for flexible development workflows, including just-in-time (JIT) compilation during development and ahead-of-time (AOT) compilation for optimized performance in production.

2. **Object-Oriented**: Dart is a pure object-

oriented language with classes and single inheritance. Everything in Dart is an object, even numbers and functions.

3. **Strong Typing**: Dart supports both static and dynamic typing. Developers can specify types explicitly, which helps catch errors at compile time, or use dynamic typing for more flexibility.

4. **Concurrency with Isolates**: Dart uses isolates, independent memory heaps, for concurrency. Isolates allow for parallel execution of code without shared memory, reducing the complexity of managing state and avoiding race conditions.

5. **Asynchronous Programming**: Dart has strong support for asynchronous programming using async-await syntax, making it easier to write non-blocking code, which is crucial for client-side applications that interact with APIs and handle user inputs.

6. **Rich Standard Library**: Dart's standard library provides a comprehensive set of APIs for various tasks, including collections, I/O, and mathematical operations, which helps streamline development processes.

7. **Flutter Integration**: Dart is the language of choice for Flutter, a framework that allows for the development of high-performance, cross-platform applications. This integration is seamless and offers a cohesive development experience.

Dart Syntax and Basics

To get started with Dart, let's look at some of the basic syntax and concepts.

Hello World Example

Here is a simple "Hello, World!" program in Dart:

```dart
void main() {
  print('Hello, World!');
}
```

This code defines the `main` function, which is the entry point of a Dart application. The `print` function is used to output text to the console.

Variables and Data Types

Dart supports a variety of data types, including numbers, strings, booleans, lists, maps, sets, and more. Here's how you can declare variables in Dart:

```dart
```

```dart
void main() {
  int age = 30;
  double height = 5.9;
  String name = 'Alice';
  bool isStudent = true;

  print('Name: $name, Age: $age, Height: $height, Student: $isStudent');
}
```

Dart also supports type inference with the `var` keyword:

```dart
void main() {
  var age = 30;
  var height = 5.9;
  var name = 'Alice';
```

```
  var isStudent = true;

  print('Name: $name, Age: $age, Height: $height, Student: $isStudent');
}
```

Control Flow Statements

Dart includes standard control flow statements like `if`, `else`, `for`, `while`, and `switch`.

```dart
void main() {
  int score = 85;

  if (score >= 90) {
    print('A');
  } else if (score >= 80) {
```

```
    print('B');
  } else if (score >= 70) {
    print('C');
  } else {
    print('F');
  }

  for (int i = 0; i < 5; i++) {
    print(i);
  }
}
```

Functions

Functions in Dart can be defined in several ways, including using optional parameters and named parameters.

```dart
int add(int a, int b) {
  return a + b;
}

void main() {
  int sum = add(3, 5);
  print(sum); // Output: 8
}
```

Dart also supports arrow syntax for concise function definitions:

```dart
int add(int a, int b) => a + b;
```

Classes and Objects

Dart is an object-oriented language, and defining classes and creating objects is straightforward.

```dart
class Person {
  String name;
  int age;

  Person(this.name, this.age);

  void display() {
    print('Name: $name, Age: $age');
  }
}

void main() {
```

```
  var person = Person('Alice', 30);
  person.display(); // Output: Name: Alice, Age: 30
}
```

Advanced Dart Concepts

Mixins

Mixins are a way of reusing a class's code in multiple class hierarchies. They are used with the `with` keyword.

```dart
mixin Singer {
  void sing() {
    print('Singing...');
  }
```

```
}

class Musician with Singer {}

void main() {
  var musician = Musician();
  musician.sing(); // Output: Singing...
}
```

Generics

Generics allow you to create classes and functions that work with different data types while maintaining type safety.

```dart
class Box<T> {
  T content;
```

```dart
  Box(this.content);

  void display() {
    print('Content: $content');
  }
}

void main() {
  var intBox = Box<int>(123);
  intBox.display(); // Output: Content: 123

  var stringBox = Box<String>('Hello');
  stringBox.display(); // Output: Content: Hello
}
```

Asynchronous Programming

Dart's support for asynchronous programming is a key feature, especially for tasks like I/O operations and network requests.

```dart
import 'dart:async';

Future<String> fetchData() async {
  await Future.delayed(Duration(seconds: 2));
  return 'Data fetched';
}

void main() async {
  print('Fetching data...');
  String data = await fetchData();
  print(data); // Output after 2 seconds: Data fetched
```

}
```

#### Isolates

Isolates provide a way to run Dart code in parallel by using separate memory heaps.

```dart
import 'dart:isolate';

void isolateEntry(SendPort sendPort) {
  sendPort.send('Hello from isolate');
}

void main() async {
  final receivePort = ReceivePort();
  await Isolate.spawn(isolateEntry, receivePort.sendPort);

```
  receivePort.listen((message) {

    print(message); // Output: Hello from isolate

    receivePort.close();

  });
}
```

Dart Ecosystem

Pub Package Manager

Pub is Dart's package manager, similar to npm for JavaScript or pip for Python. It helps in managing dependencies and publishing packages. You can find a wide range of packages at the [Pub.dev](https://pub.dev) repository.

```yaml
dependencies:
  http: ^0.13.3
```

Dart DevTools

Dart DevTools is a suite of performance and debugging tools for Dart and Flutter. It helps developers diagnose issues, analyze code performance, and debug applications.

Cross-Platform Development with Flutter

One of Dart's major strengths is its integration with Flutter, enabling developers to create high-quality apps for multiple platforms using a single codebase. Flutter's widget-based architecture leverages Dart's capabilities, allowing for expressive and flexible UIs.

Dart in Web Development

Dart can also be used for web development. Dart web apps can be compiled to JavaScript, making them runnable in any modern web browser.

```dart
import 'dart:html';

void main() {
  querySelector('#output')?.text = 'Hello, Dart!';
}
```

Dart on the Server

Dart is not limited to client-side applications; it also performs well on the server side. The `dart:io` library provides support for server-side applications, allowing for handling HTTP requests, working with files, and more.

```dart
import 'dart:io';

void main() {
  var server = HttpServer.bind('localhost', 8080);
  server.then((HttpServer srv) {
    srv.listen((HttpRequest req) {
      req.response.write('Hello from Dart server!');
      req.response.close();
    });
  });
}
```

```

### Future of Dart

The future of Dart looks promising, especially with the continuous growth of Flutter. Google's commitment to Dart ensures ongoing development and improvements. The language's evolving features and growing ecosystem make it a compelling choice for a wide range of applications.

Dart is a powerful and flexible programming language that has grown significantly since its inception. Whether you are developing for mobile, web, or server, Dart offers a robust set of features and tools to streamline the development process. Its strong typing, asynchronous capabilities, and seamless integration with Flutter make it an excellent choice for modern application development. As the language and its ecosystem continue to evolve, Dart is poised to play an increasingly important role in the future of software
```

development.

2.Guide to Installing Dart

Dart is a powerful, flexible programming language developed by Google, designed for building web, mobile, and server applications. This guide will take you through the process of installing Dart on various operating systems, setting up your development environment, and getting started with your first Dart application.

System Requirements

Before you begin, ensure your system meets the following requirements:

- **Operating System**: Windows, macOS,

or Linux

- **Memory**: At least 4GB of RAM

- **Disk Space**: Minimum 200MB free space

Installing Dart on Windows

Step 1: Download the Dart SDK

1. Visit the [official Dart SDK download page](https://dart.dev/get-dart).
2. Under the "Get the Dart SDK" section, choose the Windows tab.
3. Download the Dart SDK `.zip` file.

Step 2: Extract the Dart SDK

1. Extract the contents of the downloaded `.zip` file to a location of your choice, such as `C:\Dart`.

Step 3: Set Up Environment Variables

1. Right-click on `This PC` or `Computer` on your desktop or in File Explorer, and select `Properties`.

2. Click on `Advanced system settings` on the left panel.

3. In the System Properties window, click on the `Environment Variables` button.

4. Under `System variables`, find the `Path` variable and click `Edit`.

5. Click `New` and add the path to the `bin` directory inside the Dart SDK folder, e.g., `C:\Dart\dart-sdk\bin`.

6. Click `OK` to close all dialogs.

Step 4: Verify the Installation

1. Open a new Command Prompt window (cmd).

2. Type `dart --version` and press Enter.

3. You should see the Dart SDK version information, confirming that Dart is installed correctly.

Installing Dart on macOS

Step 1: Using Homebrew (Recommended)

Homebrew is a popular package manager for macOS. If you don't have Homebrew installed, install it by running the following command in your Terminal:

```sh
/bin/bash -c "$(curl -fsSL https://raw.githubusercontent.com/Homebrew/install/HEAD/install.sh)"
```

2. Install Dart

1. Open a Terminal window.

2. Run the following command to install Dart:

```sh
brew tap dart-lang/dart
brew install dart
```

Step 3: Verify the Installation

1. Type `dart --version` in the Terminal and press Enter.

2. You should see the Dart SDK version information, indicating that Dart is installed correctly.

Installing Dart on Linux

Step 1: Adding the Dart APT Repository (Debian/Ubuntu)

1. Open a Terminal window.

2. Run the following commands to add the Dart APT repository and install the Dart SDK:

```sh
sudo apt-get update

sudo apt-get install apt-transport-https

sudo sh -c 'wget -qO- https://dl-ssl.google.com/linux/linux_signing_key.pub | apt-key add -'

sudo sh -c 'wget -qO- https://storage.googleapis.com/download.dartlang.org/linux/debian/dart_stable.list > /etc/apt/sources.list.d/dart_stable.list'

sudo apt-get update

sudo apt-get install dart
```

```

#### Step 2: Adding Dart to Your Path

1. Open the `.bashrc` file in your home directory with a text editor, e.g., `nano ~/.bashrc`.

2. Add the following line to include Dart in your system path:

```sh
export PATH="$PATH:/usr/lib/dart/bin"
```

3. Save the file and run `source ~/.bashrc` to apply the changes.

Step 3: Verify the Installation
```

1. Type `dart --version` in the Terminal and press Enter.

2. You should see the Dart SDK version information, confirming that Dart is installed correctly.

Setting Up a Dart Development Environment

After installing Dart, you'll want to set up a development environment to write and run Dart code efficiently. Here's how to set up Dart with popular IDEs.

Using Visual Studio Code (VS Code)

Visual Studio Code is a popular code editor with excellent support for Dart.

1. Download and install [Visual Studio Code](https://code.visualstudio.com/).

2. Open Visual Studio Code.

3. Go to the Extensions view by clicking the Extensions icon in the Activity Bar on the side of the window or pressing `Ctrl+Shift+X`.

4. Search for `Dart` and click `Install` on the Dart extension by Dart Code.

Configuring VS Code for Dart

1. After installing the Dart extension, open the Command Palette (`Ctrl+Shift+P`).

2. Type `>Dart: New Project` and press Enter.

3. Select `Console Application` to create a new Dart console app.

4. Choose a location to save your project and give it a name.

5. VS Code will create a new Dart project and open the `main.dart` file for you.

Creating Your First Dart Application

Now that you have Dart installed and your development environment set up, let's create a simple Dart application.

Step 1: Create a New Dart Project

If you're using VS Code, you can follow the steps in the previous section to create a new Dart project. Alternatively, you can create a Dart project manually.

1. Open a Terminal or Command Prompt.

2. Navigate to the directory where you want to create your project.

3. Run the following command to create a new Dart project:

```sh
dart create my_first_dart_app
```

```

4. Navigate to the project directory:

```sh
cd my_first_dart_app
```

Step 2: Writing Your First Dart Program

Open the `main.dart` file located in the `bin` directory of your project. Replace the existing code with the following simple Dart program:

```dart
void main() {
  print('Hello, World!');
}
```
```

This program defines the `main` function, which is the entry point of a Dart application, and prints "Hello, World!" to the console.

Step 3: Running Your Dart Program

1. Open a Terminal or Command Prompt.

2. Navigate to the directory of your Dart project.

3. Run the following command to execute your Dart program:

```sh
dart run bin/main.dart
```

You should see the output "Hello, World!" printed to the console.

Managing Packages with Pub

Dart's package manager, Pub, allows you to easily manage dependencies and packages in your Dart projects. Here's how to use Pub to add dependencies to your project.

Step 1: Adding Dependencies

1. Open the `pubspec.yaml` file in the root directory of your Dart project.

2. Add dependencies under the `dependencies` section. For example, to add the `http` package, modify your `pubspec.yaml` file as follows:

```yaml
name: my_first_dart_app

description: A simple Dart application.

version: 1.0.0
```

environment:
  sdk: '>=2.12.0 <3.0.0'

dependencies:
  http: ^0.13.3
```

3. Save the `pubspec.yaml` file.

#### Step 2: Installing Dependencies

1. Open a Terminal or Command Prompt in your project directory.

2. Run the following command to install the dependencies:

```sh
dart pub get

```

Additional Resources

To further explore Dart, consider the following resources:

- **Official Dart Documentation**: dart.dev

- **Dart Language Tour**: [Language Tour](https://dart.dev/guides/language/language-tour)

- **Dart Packages**: pub.dev

- **Dart and Flutter Community**: Engage with the community on forums, Discord, and GitHub.

Installing Dart is a straightforward process on any major operating system. By following this guide, you've set up Dart on your machine,
```

configured a development environment, and written and executed your first Dart program. With Dart installed and your environment ready, you're now prepared to explore the language's full potential and start building powerful applications. Whether you're developing for the web, mobile, or server-side, Dart provides a versatile and robust platform for your development needs.

3.Using an IDE for Dart with Examples

Introduction

Using an Integrated Development Environment (IDE) can significantly enhance your Dart programming experience. IDEs provide various tools and features like syntax highlighting, code completion, debugging, and more. This guide will walk you through setting up and using Visual Studio Code (VS Code) and IntelliJ IDEA, two popular IDEs for Dart development, with detailed examples.

Visual Studio Code (VS Code)

Installation

1. **Download and Install VS Code**:

   - Visit the [Visual Studio Code download page](https://code.visualstudio.com/).

- Download and install the version suitable for your operating system.

2. **Install Dart and Flutter Extensions**:

   - Open VS Code.

   - Go to the Extensions view by clicking the Extensions icon in the Activity Bar on the side of the window or pressing `Ctrl+Shift+X`.

   - Search for `Dart` and click `Install` on the Dart extension by Dart Code.

   - If you plan to use Flutter, search for `Flutter` and install the Flutter extension as well.

Setting Up a Dart Project

1. **Create a New Dart Project**:

   - Open the Command Palette (`Ctrl+Shift+P`).

   - Type `>Dart: New Project` and press Enter.

- Select `Console Application` to create a new Dart console app.

  - Choose a location to save your project and give it a name.

  - VS Code will create a new Dart project and open the `main.dart` file for you.

2. **Write a Simple Dart Program**:

   - Open the `main.dart` file located in the `bin` directory of your project.

   - Replace the existing code with the following:

```dart
void main() {
  print('Hello, Dart with VS Code!');
}
```

3. **Run the Dart Program**:

- Open the Terminal in VS Code (`Ctrl+``).

- Navigate to the project directory if not already there.

- Run the program with the following command:

```sh
dart run bin/main.dart
```

- You should see the output `Hello, Dart with VS Code!` printed in the terminal.

Debugging in VS Code

1. **Set a Breakpoint**:

    - Open the `main.dart` file.

    - Click in the gutter to the left of the line number where you want to set a breakpoint (e.g., on the `print` statement).

2. **Start Debugging**:

   - Open the Run and Debug view by clicking the play icon in the Activity Bar on the side of the window or pressing `Ctrl+Shift+D`.

   - Click the green play button or press `F5` to start debugging.

   - The debugger will stop at the breakpoint, allowing you to inspect variables and step through the code.

IntelliJ IDEA

Installation

1. **Download and Install IntelliJ IDEA**:

   - Visit the [IntelliJ IDEA download page] (https://www.jetbrains.com/idea/download/).

   - Download and install the Community or Ultimate edition.

2. **Install Dart Plugin**:

   - Open IntelliJ IDEA.

   - Go to `File` > `Settings` (or `Preferences` on macOS).

   - In the Settings/Preferences dialog, select `Plugins`.

   - Search for `Dart` and install the Dart plugin.

Setting Up a Dart Project

1. **Create a New Dart Project**:

   - Open IntelliJ IDEA and click on `Create New Project`.

   - Select `Dart` in the project type list.

   - Set the project location and click `Create`.

2. **Write a Simple Dart Program**:

- IntelliJ IDEA creates a basic project structure with a `main.dart` file.

- Open the `main.dart` file.

- Replace the existing code with the following:

```dart
void main() {
  print('Hello, Dart with IntelliJ IDEA!');
}
```

3. **Run the Dart Program**:

   - Right-click on the `main.dart` file and select `Run 'main.dart'`.

   - You should see the output `Hello, Dart with IntelliJ IDEA!` in the Run window.

Debugging in IntelliJ IDEA

1. **Set a Breakpoint**:

   - Open the `main.dart` file.

   - Click in the gutter to the left of the line number where you want to set a breakpoint (e.g., on the `print` statement).

2. **Start Debugging**:

   - Right-click on the `main.dart` file and select `Debug 'main.dart'`.

   - The debugger will stop at the breakpoint, allowing you to inspect variables and step through the code.

Using Dart DevTools

Dart DevTools is a suite of performance and debugging tools for Dart and Flutter. It can be used with both VS Code and IntelliJ IDEA.

Running Dart DevTools with VS Code

1. **Install Dart DevTools**:

   - If you have the Dart and Flutter extensions installed, Dart DevTools is already included.

2. **Launch Dart DevTools**:

   - Run your Dart application in debug mode.

   - After starting the application, you should see a link to Dart DevTools in the Debug Console. Click on this link to open Dart DevTools in your web browser.

Running Dart DevTools with IntelliJ IDEA

1. **Install Dart DevTools**:

   - Ensure that you have the Dart plugin installed.

2. **Launch Dart DevTools**:

   - Run your Dart application in debug mode.

   - In the Run window, you will see a link to Dart DevTools. Click on this link to open Dart DevTools in your web browser.

Example: Building a Simple Command-Line Application

Let's build a simple command-line application that takes user input and prints a response.

1. **Create a New Dart Project**:

   - Follow the steps in your chosen IDE to create a new Dart console application.

2. **Write the Application Code**:

   - Open the `main.dart` file and replace the existing code with the following:

```dart
import 'dart:io';

void main() {
  stdout.write('Enter your name: ');
  String? name = stdin.readLineSync();
  print('Hello, $name!');
}
```

3. **Run the Application**:

   - Run the application from your IDE.

   - The program will prompt you to enter your name and then greet you.

Example: Building a Simple Web Server

For more advanced usage, you can build a simple web server using Dart. This example will demonstrate how to create a web server that responds with "Hello, Dart!" to any request.

1. **Create a New Dart Project**:

   - Follow the steps in your chosen IDE to create a new Dart console application.

2. **Add HTTP Package**:

   - Open the `pubspec.yaml` file and add the `http` package under dependencies:

```yaml
dependencies:
  http: ^0.13.3
```

   - Run `dart pub get` to install the package.

3. **Write the Web Server Code**:

   - Open the `main.dart` file and replace the existing code with the following:

```dart
import 'dart:io';

Future<void> main() async {
  final server = await HttpServer.bind(InternetAddress.loopbackIPv4, 8080);
  print('Server running on http://${server.address.address}:${server.port}');

  await for (HttpRequest request in server) {
    request.response
      ..write('Hello, Dart!')
      ..close();
  }
```

}
```

4. **Run the Web Server**:

    - Run the application from your IDE.

    - Open a web browser and navigate to `http://localhost:8080`.

    - You should see the message "Hello, Dart!" displayed in the browser.

Using an IDE like Visual Studio Code or IntelliJ IDEA can greatly enhance your Dart development experience. These IDEs provide robust features such as syntax highlighting, code completion, debugging, and integration with Dart DevTools. By following the examples provided, you can set up a Dart project, write and run Dart code, and even build more complex applications like command-line tools and web servers. With these tools at your disposal, you're well-equipped to take full advantage of Dart's
```

capabilities.

4. Basic Syntax of Dart: Variable Declaration with Examples

Understanding how to declare and use variables is fundamental in any programming language. In Dart, variables can be declared in several ways depending on their intended use. This guide will explain the different types of variable declarations in Dart, including mutable and immutable variables, as well as type annotations and type inference. We will also provide examples to illustrate each concept.

Declaring Variables in Dart

Mutable Variables

Mutable variables are those whose values can change after they are initially set. In Dart, you can declare a mutable variable using the `var` keyword or by explicitly specifying the type.

Using `var`

The `var` keyword allows Dart to infer the type of the variable based on the assigned value. Here's an example:

```dart
void main() {
  var name = 'Alice'; // Dart infers that name is a String
  print(name); // Output: Alice

  name = 'Bob'; // Changing the value of the variable
  print(name); // Output: Bob
}
```

Specifying the Type

You can also explicitly specify the type of the variable when declaring it. This makes your code more readable and helps catch type errors at compile time.

```dart
void main() {
  String name = 'Alice';
  print(name); // Output: Alice

  name = 'Bob';
  print(name); // Output: Bob
}
```

Immutable Variables

Immutable variables are those whose values

cannot change once they are set. In Dart, you can declare immutable variables using the `final` or `const` keywords.

Using `final`

The `final` keyword is used to declare a variable that can only be set once. The value of a `final` variable can be determined at runtime.

```dart
void main() {
  final name = 'Alice';
  print(name); // Output: Alice

  // name = 'Bob'; // This line would cause an error because final variables cannot be reassigned
}
```

```

##### Using `const`

The `const` keyword is used to declare compile-time constants. The value of a `const` variable must be known at compile time and cannot change.

```dart
void main() {
  const name = 'Alice';
  print(name); // Output: Alice

  // name = 'Bob'; // This line would cause an error because const variables cannot be reassigned
}
```
```

Type Annotations and Type Inference

Dart is a statically typed language, which means that the type of a variable is known at compile time. You can explicitly specify the type of a variable or let Dart infer the type based on the assigned value.

Type Annotations

Type annotations help make your code more readable and can prevent type-related errors. Here are some examples of using type annotations:

```dart
void main() {
  int age = 30;
  double height = 5.9;
  bool isStudent = true;
```

```dart
  String greeting = 'Hello, Dart!';

  print('Age: $age'); // Output: Age: 30
  print('Height: $height'); // Output: Height: 5.9
  print('Is student: $isStudent'); // Output: Is student: true
  print('Greeting: $greeting'); // Output: Greeting: Hello, Dart!
}
```

Type Inference

When you use the `var` keyword, Dart infers the type of the variable based on the assigned value. Here are some examples:

```dart
void main() {
```

```
  var age = 30; // Dart infers that age is an int

  var height = 5.9; // Dart infers that height is a double

  var isStudent = true; // Dart infers that isStudent is a bool

  var greeting = 'Hello, Dart!'; // Dart infers that greeting is a String


  print('Age: $age'); // Output: Age: 30

  print('Height: $height'); // Output: Height: 5.9

  print('Is student: $isStudent'); // Output: Is student: true

  print('Greeting: $greeting'); // Output: Greeting: Hello, Dart!

}
```

Nullable and Non-nullable Variables

In Dart, you can specify whether a variable can be null by using a question mark (`?`) after the type. By default, variables are non-nullable, meaning they cannot hold a `null` value unless explicitly declared as nullable.

Non-nullable Variables

Non-nullable variables cannot hold a `null` value and must be initialized before they are used.

```dart
void main() {
  int age = 30;
  print('Age: $age'); // Output: Age: 30

  // int? height; // This would cause an error if accessed before being initialized
}
```

```

#### Nullable Variables

Nullable variables can hold a `null` value. You declare a nullable variable by adding a question mark (`?`) after the type.

```dart
void main() {
  int? age;
  print('Age: $age'); // Output: Age: null

  age = 30;
  print('Age: $age'); // Output: Age: 30
}
```

Late Initialization
```

Dart provides the `late` keyword, which allows you to initialize a non-nullable variable after its declaration. This can be useful for variables that depend on some computation or external input.

```dart
void main() {
  late int age;

  // Perform some computation
  age = 30;

  print('Age: $age'); // Output: Age: 30
}
```

Variable Scope

The scope of a variable determines where it can be accessed in your code. Dart has two main types of scope: local scope and global scope.

Local Scope

Variables declared inside a function or a block (such as an if statement or a loop) have local scope and can only be accessed within that function or block.

```dart
void main() {
  int age = 30; // Local scope to main function

  if (age > 20) {
    String message = 'You are an adult'; // Local scope to if block
    print(message); // Output: You are an adult
```

}

  // print(message); // This would cause an error because message is not accessible outside the if block
}
```

#### Global Scope

Variables declared outside any function or block have global scope and can be accessed from anywhere in the file.

```dart
int age = 30; // Global scope

void main() {
  print('Age: $age'); // Output: Age: 30

```
  updateAge();

  print('Updated Age: $age'); // Output: Updated Age: 35

}


void updateAge() {

  age = 35; // Accessing and modifying global variable

}
```

Understanding how to declare and use variables is crucial for mastering Dart. This guide covered the basics of variable declaration, including mutable and immutable variables, type annotations and type inference, nullable and non-nullable variables, late initialization, and variable scope. By following these examples, you should be well-equipped to use variables effectively in your Dart programs.

5. Operators in Dart with Examples

Introduction

Operators are special symbols that perform specific operations on one or more operands. Dart supports a wide range of operators, including arithmetic, relational, logical, bitwise, assignment, and more. Understanding these operators is crucial for writing efficient and effective Dart code. This guide will cover various operators in Dart with detailed examples.

Arithmetic Operators

Arithmetic operators are used to perform basic mathematical operations such as addition, subtraction, multiplication, division, and modulus.

- **Addition (`+`)**: Adds two operands.

```dart
void main() {
  int a = 10;
  int b = 5;
  int sum = a + b;
  print('Sum: $sum'); // Output: Sum: 15
}
```

- **Subtraction (`-`)**: Subtracts the second operand from the first.

```dart
void main() {
  int a = 10;
  int b = 5;
  int difference = a - b;
```

print('Difference: $difference'); // Output: Difference: 5

  }
  ```

- **Multiplication (`*`)**: Multiplies two operands.

  ```dart
  void main() {
    int a = 10;
    int b = 5;
    int product = a * b;
    print('Product: $product'); // Output: Product: 50
  }
  ```

- **Division (`/`)**: Divides the first operand
  ```

by the second and returns a double.

```dart
void main() {
  int a = 10;
  int b = 5;
  double quotient = a / b;
  print('Quotient: $quotient'); // Output: Quotient: 2.0
}
```

- **Integer Division (`~/`)**: Divides the first operand by the second and returns an integer.

```dart
void main() {
  int a = 10;
  int b = 3;
```

```dart
int quotient = a ~/ b;

print('Integer Quotient: $quotient'); // Output: Integer Quotient: 3
}
```

- **Modulus (`%`)**: Returns the remainder of the division of the first operand by the second.

```dart
void main() {
  int a = 10;
  int b = 3;
  int remainder = a % b;
  print('Remainder: $remainder'); // Output: Remainder: 1
}
```

Relational Operators

Relational operators are used to compare two values. They return a boolean result.

- **Equal to (`==`)**: Checks if two operands are equal.

```dart
void main() {
  int a = 10;
  int b = 10;
  print(a == b); // Output: true
}
```

- **Not equal to (`!=`)**: Checks if two operands are not equal.

```dart
void main() {
  int a = 10;
  int b = 5;
  print(a != b); // Output: true
}
```

- **Greater than (`>`)**: Checks if the first operand is greater than the second.

```dart
void main() {
  int a = 10;
  int b = 5;
  print(a > b); // Output: true
}
```

- **Less than (`<`)**: Checks if the first operand is less than the second.

```dart
void main() {
  int a = 10;
  int b = 5;
  print(a < b); // Output: false
}
```

- **Greater than or equal to (`>=`)**: Checks if the first operand is greater than or equal to the second.

```dart
void main() {
```

```
  int a = 10;
  int b = 5;
  print(a >= b); // Output: true
}
```

- **Less than or equal to (`<=`)**: Checks if the first operand is less than or equal to the second.

```dart
void main() {
  int a = 10;
  int b = 5;
  print(a <= b); // Output: false
}
```

Logical Operators

Logical operators are used to combine multiple boolean expressions or to negate a boolean expression.

- **AND (`&&`)**: Returns true if both operands are true.

```dart
void main() {
  bool a = true;
  bool b = false;
  print(a && b); // Output: false
}
```

- **OR (`||`)**: Returns true if at least one of the operands is true.

```dart
void main() {
  bool a = true;
  bool b = false;
  print(a || b); // Output: true
}
```

- **NOT (`!`)**: Returns true if the operand is false and vice versa.

```dart
void main() {
  bool a = true;
  print(!a); // Output: false
}
```

Bitwise Operators

Bitwise operators perform operations on the binary representations of numbers.

- **AND (`&`)**: Performs a bitwise AND operation.

```dart
void main() {
  int a = 5; // 0101 in binary
  int b = 3; // 0011 in binary
  print(a & b); // Output: 1 (0001 in binary)
}
```

- **OR (`|`)**: Performs a bitwise OR operation.

```dart
void main() {
  int a = 5; // 0101 in binary
  int b = 3; // 0011 in binary
  print(a | b); // Output: 7 (0111 in binary)
}
```

- **XOR (`^`)**: Performs a bitwise XOR operation.

```dart
void main() {
  int a = 5; // 0101 in binary
  int b = 3; // 0011 in binary
  print(a ^ b); // Output: 6 (0110 in binary)
}
```

- **NOT (`~`)**: Performs a bitwise NOT operation.

```dart
void main() {
  int a = 5; // 0101 in binary
  print(~a); // Output: -6 (Inverts all bits)
}
```

- **Left shift (`<<`)**: Shifts the bits of the first operand to the left by the number of positions specified by the second operand.

```dart
void main() {
  int a = 5; // 0101 in binary
  print(a << 1); // Output: 10 (1010 in binary)
```

    }
    ```

- **Right shift (`>>`)**: Shifts the bits of the first operand to the right by the number of positions specified by the second operand.

    ```dart
    void main() {
      int a = 5; // 0101 in binary
      print(a >> 1); // Output: 2 (0010 in binary)
    }
    ```

Assignment Operators

Assignment operators are used to assign values to variables. Dart supports a variety of assignment operators.
    ```

- **Simple assignment (`=`)**: Assigns the value of the right operand to the left operand.

```dart
void main() {
  int a = 10;
  print(a); // Output: 10
}
```

- **Add and assign (`+=`)**: Adds the right operand to the left operand and assigns the result to the left operand.

```dart
void main() {
  int a = 10;
  a += 5; // Equivalent to a = a + 5;
```

```
  print(a); // Output: 15
}
```

- **Subtract and assign (`-=`)**: Subtracts the right operand from the left operand and assigns the result to the left operand.

```dart
void main() {
  int a = 10;
  a -= 5; // Equivalent to a = a - 5;
  print(a); // Output: 5
}
```

- **Multiply and assign (`*=`)**: Multiplies the left operand by the right operand and assigns the result to the left operand.

```dart
void main() {
  int a = 10;
  a *= 5; // Equivalent to a = a * 5;
  print(a); // Output: 50
}
```

- **Divide and assign (`/=`)**: Divides the left operand by the right operand and assigns the result to the left operand.

```dart
void main() {
  double a = 10;
  a /= 5; // Equivalent to a = a / 5;
  print(a); // Output: 2.0
}
```

```

- **Modulus and assign (`%=`)**: Computes the modulus of the left operand by the right operand and assigns the result to the left operand.

```dart
void main() {
  int a = 10;
  a %= 3; // Equivalent to a = a % 3;
  print(a); // Output: 1
}
```

Conditional Expressions

Dart provides conditional expressions that evaluate expressions based on a condition.
```

- **Ternary operator (`?:`)**: The ternary operator is a shorthand for if-else statements.

```dart
void main() {
  int a = 10;
  int b = 5;
  String result = a > b ? 'a is greater' : 'b is greater';
  print(result); // Output: a is greater
}
```

- **Null-aware operators**: Dart offers operators that are useful when working with nullable types.

- **Null-aware assignment (`??=`)**: Assigns a value to a variable only if it is null.

```dart
void main() {
  int? a;
  a ??= 5; // Assigns 5 to a because it is null
  print(a); // Output: 5
}
```

- **Null-aware access (`?.`)**: Accesses a member only if the object is not null.

```dart
void main() {
  String? name;
  print(name?.length); // Output: null
```

}
  ```

- **Null-coalescing operator (`??`)**: Returns the right operand if the left operand is null.

  ```dart
  void main() {
    String? name;
    print(name ?? 'Guest'); // Output: Guest
  }
  ```

Type Test Operators

Type test operators are used to check the type of an object at runtime.
  ```

- **`is`**: Checks if an object is of a specific type.

```dart
void main() {
  int a = 10;
  print(a is int); // Output: true
  print(a is String); // Output: false
}
```

- **`is!`**: Checks if an object is not of a specific type.

```dart
void main() {
  int a = 10;
  print(a is! int); // Output: false
  print(a is! String); // Output: true
```

}
```

### Summary

Dart provides a rich set of operators to perform various operations on data. This guide covered arithmetic, relational, logical, bitwise, assignment, conditional, and type test operators with detailed examples. Understanding and using these operators effectively is essential for writing robust and efficient Dart code. By mastering these operators, you'll be well-equipped to handle a wide range of programming tasks in Dart.
```

6. Control structures in Dart

Control structures in Dart are essential tools for programming, allowing developers to manage the flow of their code and make decisions based on certain conditions. In this guide, we will explore the various control structures available in Dart, including if statements, for loops, while loops, switch cases, and try-catch blocks.

1. If statements:

If statements are used to execute a block of code only if a specified condition is true. They have the following syntax in Dart:

```
if (condition) {
  // code to be executed if the condition is true
} else {
```

// code to be executed if the condition is false
}
```

Here's an example of an if statement in Dart:

```
int number = 10;

if (number > 5) {
  print('The number is greater than 5');
} else {
  print('The number is less than or equal to 5');
}
```

2. For loops:
```

For loops are used to iterate over a sequence of elements a specific number of times. They have the following syntax in Dart:

```
for (initialization; condition; increment) {
  // code to be executed for each iteration
}
```

Here's an example of a for loop in Dart:

```
for (int i = 0; i < 5; i++) {
  print('Count: $i');
}
```

3. While loops:

While loops are used to execute a block of code as long as a specified condition is true. They have the following syntax in Dart:

```
while (condition) {
  // code to be executed while the condition is true
}
```

Here's an example of a while loop in Dart:

```
int i = 0;

while (i < 5) {
  print('Count: $i');
```

```
  i++;
}
```

4. Switch cases:

Switch cases are used to execute different blocks of code based on the value of a variable. They have the following syntax in Dart:

```
switch (expression) {
  case value1:
    // code to be executed if the expression is equal to value1
    break;
  case value2:
    // code to be executed if the expression is equal to value2
```

```
    break;
  default:
    // code to be executed if the expression doesn't match any case
}
```

Here's an example of a switch case in Dart:

```
String fruit = 'apple';

switch (fruit) {
  case 'apple':
    print('It is an apple');
    break;
  case 'banana':
    print('It is a banana');
```

```
    break;
  default:
    print('Unknown fruit');
}
```

5. Try-catch blocks:

Try-catch blocks are used to handle exceptions that may occur during the execution of code. They have the following syntax in Dart:

```
try {
  // code that may throw an exception
} catch (e) {
  // code to handle the exception
}
```

```

Here's an example of a try-catch block in Dart:

```
try {
  int result = 10 ~/ 0; // division by zero
  print('Result: $result');
} catch (e) {
  print('An error occurred: $e');
}
```

In this guide, we have explored the various control structures available in Dart, including if statements, for loops, while loops, switch cases, and try-catch blocks. These structures are essential tools for developers to manage the flow of their code and make decisions
```

based on certain conditions.

7.Dart, functions

In Dart, functions are blocks of code that are used to perform a specific task. They can take in parameters and return a value. Functions are a fundamental part of programming in Dart, as they help in organizing code and making it more modular.

Here are some examples of how functions work in Dart:

1. Declaring a function:

To declare a function in Dart, you use the keyword "void" if the function does not return a value, or the type of value that the function returns. Here is an example of a function that takes in two parameters and returns the sum of the two numbers:

```dart
```

```dart
int add(int a, int b) {
  return a + b;
}
```

In this example, the function "add" takes in two parameters "a" and "b" of type int, and returns the sum of these two numbers.

2. Calling a function:

To call a function in Dart, you simply use the function name followed by parentheses, with any required arguments inside the parentheses. Here is an example of calling the "add" function from the previous example:

```dart
int result = add(3, 4);
print(result); // Output: 7
```

```

In this example, we are calling the "add" function with arguments 3 and 4, and storing the result in a variable "result".

3. Optional parameters:

In Dart, you can define optional parameters for a function by enclosing them in square brackets []. Optional parameters do not have to be provided when calling the function. Here is an example of a function with an optional parameter:

```dart
void greet(String name, [String greeting = 'Hello']) {
  print('$greeting, $name!');
}
```
```

In this example, the function "greet" has an optional parameter "greeting" with a default value of 'Hello'. You can call this function without providing a value for the optional parameter:

```dart
greet('John'); // Output: Hello, John!
greet('Jane', 'Hi'); // Output: Hi, Jane!
```

4. Named parameters:

Dart also supports named parameters, which allows you to specify parameters by their names when calling the function. Named parameters are enclosed in curly braces {}. Here is an example of a function with named parameters:

```dart
void introduce({String name, int age}) {
  print('My name is $name and I am $age years old.');
}
```

In this example, the function "introduce" has two named parameters "name" and "age". You can call this function by specifying the parameter names:

```dart
introduce(name: 'Alice', age: 30); // Output: My name is Alice and I am 30 years old.
```

5. Anonymous functions:

In Dart, you can also define functions without

a name, known as anonymous functions or lambda functions. These functions are useful for quick tasks or as arguments to higher-order functions. Here is an example of an anonymous function:

```dart
List<String> cities = ['New York', 'London', 'Paris'];

cities.forEach((city) {
  print(city);
});
```

In this example, we are using an anonymous function as an argument to the "forEach" method of the List class. The anonymous function takes in a parameter "city" and prints it to the console.

Control structures in Dart:

Control structures allow you to control the flow of execution in a program by making decisions and repeating blocks of code based on certain conditions. In Dart, there are several control structures available, such as if statements, loops, switch statements, and more.

1. If statements:

If statements are used to execute a block of code only if a certain condition is true. You can also use else if and else clauses to handle multiple conditions. Here is an example of an if statement in Dart:

```dart
int age = 25;
```

```
if (age >= 18) {
  print('You are an adult.');
} else {
  print('You are a minor.');
}
```

In this example, the code inside the if block is executed if the condition (age >= 18) is true, otherwise the code inside the else block is executed.

2. Loops:

Loops are used to execute a block of code repeatedly until a certain condition is met. Dart provides several types of loops, such as for loops, while loops, and do-while loops. Here is an example of a for loop in Dart:

```dart
for (int i = 0; i < 5; i++) {
  print('Count: $i');
}
```

In this example, the for loop will execute the code inside the loop body 5 times, starting from 0 and incrementing the value of i by 1 in each iteration.

3. Switch statements:

Switch statements are used to select one of many code blocks to be executed based on the value of an expression. Dart switch statements can also have default cases to handle values that do not match any of the cases. Here is an example of a switch statement in Dart:

```dart
String day = 'Monday';

switch (day) {
  case 'Monday':
    print('Start of the week');
    break;
  case 'Friday':
    print('End of the week');
    break;
  default:
    print('Another day');
}
```

In this example, the switch statement checks the value of the variable "day" and prints a message based on the case that matches the value.

These are some of the basic functions and control structures in Dart. By leveraging functions and control structures effectively, you can write more organized and efficient code in Dart.

8. Object-oriented programming (OOP) in Dart

Object-oriented programming (OOP) in Dart is a popular programming paradigm that focuses on creating objects and classes to organize code and data. This approach allows for the encapsulation, inheritance, and polymorphism of objects, making code easier to manage and maintain.

One of the main concepts in OOP is the class. A class is a blueprint for creating objects that defines the properties and behaviors of those objects. For example, we can create a class in Dart called "Person" with properties like name, age, and gender, and behaviors like walking and talking.

```
class Person {
  String name;
  int age;
  String gender;

  void walk() {
```

```
  print('$name is walking');
  }

  void talk(String message) {
    print('$name says: $message');
  }
}
```

To create an object of the class Person, we instantiate it by using the `new` keyword:

```
Person person1 = new Person();
person1.name = 'Alice';
person1.age = 30;
person1.gender = 'female';

person1.walk();
person1.talk('Hello, world!');
```

Inheritance is another important concept in OOP that allows classes to inherit properties and methods from other classes. In Dart, we can achieve inheritance using the `extends` keyword. For example, we can create a class called "Employee" that extends the class Person:

```
class Employee extends Person {
  String jobTitle;
  double salary;

  void work() {
    print('$name is working as a $jobTitle');
  }
}
```

Now, the Employee class inherits all the properties and methods from the Person class. We can create an object of the Employee class and access all the inherited properties and methods:

```
Employee employee1 = new Employee();
employee1.name = 'Bob';
employee1.age = 25;
employee1.gender = 'male';
employee1.jobTitle = 'Software Engineer';
employee1.salary = 75000.0;
```

```
employee1.walk();
employee1.talk('Good morning!');
employee1.work();
```

Polymorphism is the ability for objects of different classes to be treated as objects of a common superclass. In Dart, polymorphism can be achieved through method overriding. For example, we can override the `talk` method in the Employee class to provide a specific implementation:

```
class Employee extends Person {
  // existing properties and methods

  @override
  void talk(String message) {
    print('$name, the $jobTitle, says: $message');
  }
}
```

Now, when we call the `talk` method on an

object of the Employee class, the overridden implementation will be used:

```
Employee employee1 = new Employee();
// set properties
employee1.talk('How can I help you today?'); // output: Bob, the Software Engineer, says: How can I help you today?
```

Encapsulation is the practice of bundling the data and methods that operate on the data within a single unit, such as a class. This helps in hiding the implementation details and only exposing the necessary interfaces to interact with objects. In Dart, we can achieve encapsulation by using access modifiers like `public`, `private`, and `protected`. By default, all members in a Dart class are `public`, but we can use the underscore (`_`) prefix to make a member `private`.

For example, we can modify the Person class to have private properties like so:

```
```

```dart
class Person {
  String _name;
  int _age;
  String _gender;

  Person(this._name, this._age, this._gender);

  void walk() {
    print('$_name is walking');
  }

  void talk(String message) {
    print('$_name says: $message');
  }

  int get age => _age;

  set age(int value) => _age = value;
}
```

In this modified version, the properties `_name`, `_age`, and `_gender` are private and can only be accessed within the class. We have also added a constructor to initialize these properties and getter and setter methods to access and modify the private properties.

```
Person person2 = new Person('Charlie', 40, 'male');
person2.walk(); // output: Charlie is walking
print(person2.age); // output: 40
person2.age = 45;
print(person2.age); // output: 45
```

Overall, object-oriented programming in Dart provides a powerful way to structure and organize code by creating reusable objects and classes. By understanding and applying concepts like classes, inheritance, polymorphism, and encapsulation, developers can build complex and scalable applications in a more efficient and maintainable way.

9. Create classes and objects

Dart is a powerful programming language that allows you to create classes and objects to encapsulate data and behavior in your applications. In this tutorial, we will explore how to create classes and objects in Dart, along with some examples to demonstrate their usage.

Creating a class in Dart is quite simple. You can define a class using the `class` keyword, followed by the class name and a pair of curly braces to define the class body. Inside the class body, you can declare fields (variables) and methods (functions) that define the behavior of the class.

```dart
class Person {
  String name;
  int age;

  void sayHello() {
    print('Hello, my name is $name and I am
```

$age years old.');
  }
}
```

In the example above, we have defined a class called `Person` with two fields: `name` of type `String` and `age` of type `int`. We have also defined a method called `sayHello()` that prints a greeting message using the `name` and `age` fields of the `Person` object.

To create an object of a class in Dart, you can use the `new` keyword followed by the class name and parentheses to instantiate the object. You can then access the fields and methods of the object using the dot notation (`.`).

```dart
void main() {
  Person person = Person();
  person.name = 'Alice';
  person.age = 30;

```
  person.sayHello();
}
```

In this example, we have created an instance of the `Person` class called `person`, set the `name` and `age` fields of the object, and called the `sayHello()` method to print a greeting message using the object's data.

You can also define constructors in Dart to initialize the fields of a class when an object is created. Constructors in Dart are defined using the same name as the class and can take parameters to initialize the fields of the class.

```dart
class Person {
  String name;
  int age;

  Person(String name, int age) {
    this.name = name;
    this.age = age;
  }
```

```
  void sayHello() {
    print('Hello, my name is $name and I am $age years old.');
  }
}
```

In the updated `Person` class above, we have defined a constructor that takes two parameters (`name` and `age`) to initialize the fields of the `Person` object when it is created. You can then create an object of the `Person` class and pass in the required parameters to the constructor to initialize the object.

```dart
void main() {
  Person person = Person('Bob', 25);
  person.sayHello();
}
```

In the `main()` function, we have created an instance of the `Person` class called `person` and passed in the values `'Bob'` and `25` to the constructor to initialize the `name` and `age` fields of the object. We then called the `sayHello()` method to print a greeting message using the object's data.

Dart also supports inheritance, allowing you to create subclasses that inherit fields and methods from a superclass. To create a subclass in Dart, you can use the `extends` keyword followed by the superclass name to indicate that the subclass extends the superclass.

```dart
class Student extends Person {
  String major;

  Student(String name, int age, this.major) : super(name, age);
}
```

In the example above, we have defined a subclass called `Student` that extends the `Person` class. The `Student` class has an additional field called `major` to represent the student's area of study. We have also defined a constructor for the `Student` class that initializes the `name`, `age`, and `major` fields using the superclass constructor (`super(name, age)`).

```dart
void main() {
  Student student = Student('Alice', 20, 'Computer Science');
  student.sayHello();
}
```

In the `main()` function, we have created an instance of the `Student` class called `student` and passed in the values `'Alice'`, `20`, and `'Computer Science'` to the constructor to initialize the fields of the object. We then called the `sayHello()` method to print a greeting message using the object's data, demonstrating how the subclass inherits the behavior of the superclass.

In conclusion, Dart provides a flexible and powerful way to create classes and objects in your applications. By defining classes, instantiating objects, and using constructors and inheritance, you can organize and encapsulate your code to build robust and maintainable software. Experiment with creating classes and objects in Dart to unleash the full potential of the language in your projects.

10. Classes

Inheritance in Dart is a fundamental concept that allows classes to inherit properties and methods from other classes. This promotes code reusability and helps in building a more organized and modular codebase. In Dart, inheritance is implemented using the "extends" keyword.

Let's take a look at an example to better understand how inheritance works in Dart:

```dart
class Animal {
  String name;

  Animal(this.name);

  void speak() {
    print('The $name is making a sound');
  }
}

class Dog extends Animal {
  String breed;
```

```
  Dog(String name, this.breed) : super(name);

  void wagTail() {
    print('The $name is wagging its tail');
  }
}

void main() {
  Dog myDog = Dog('Buddy', 'Labrador');

  myDog.speak();
  myDog.wagTail();
}
```

In this example, we have two classes: Animal and Dog. The Animal class has a property "name" and a method "speak" which prints a generic message. The Dog class extends the Animal class, inheriting the properties and methods from it. It adds its own property "breed" and method "wagTail" which prints a specific message for dogs.

When we create an instance of the Dog class and call the "speak" and "wagTail" methods, we can see that the properties and methods of the Animal class are also accessible to the Dog class through inheritance.

Another important concept in inheritance is method overriding. This allows subclasses to provide a specific implementation for a method inherited from a superclass. Here's an example to illustrate method overriding in Dart:

```dart
class Shape {
  void draw() {
    print('Drawing a shape');
  }
}

class Circle extends Shape {
  @override
  void draw() {
    print('Drawing a circle');
  }
}

void main() {
  Circle circle = Circle();
```

```
  circle.draw();
}
```

In this example, the Circle class overrides the "draw" method inherited from the Shape class. When we create an instance of the Circle class and call the "draw" method, the specific implementation in the Circle class is executed.

Inheritance and method overriding are powerful features in Dart that help in creating more flexible and efficient code. By effectively utilizing inheritance, developers can save time and effort by reusing existing code and building upon it to create new functionalities.

11. Polymorphism in Dart

Polymorphism in Dart is the ability of a single function or method to operate on different types of data. This means that a function or method can behave differently depending on the data it is operating on. Polymorphism is one of the key principles of object-oriented programming, allowing for more flexible and reusable code.

There are two main types of polymorphism in Dart: compile-time polymorphism and runtime polymorphism.

Compile-time polymorphism, also known as method overloading, allows you to define multiple methods with the same name but different parameters. Dart will determine which method to call based on the number and types of parameters passed to it. This allows you to have multiple methods with the same name but different functionality.

For example, you could have a method called calculateArea that takes in different parameters depending on the shape being calculated. You could have calculateArea for a circle that takes in the radius, and calculateArea for a rectangle that takes in the length and width.

Runtime polymorphism, on the other hand, allows you to achieve polymorphic behavior through inheritance and method overriding. This means that a method in a superclass can be overridden in a subclass to provide specific functionality for that subclass. Dart will determine which method to call at runtime based on the actual type of the object.

For example, you could have a superclass called Shape with a method called draw. You could then have subclasses such as Circle and Rectangle that override the draw method to provide specific drawing functionality for each shape.

Polymorphism in Dart allows for more flexible and scalable code by promoting code reuse and allowing for dynamic behavior based on the data being operated on. By using polymorphism, you can write code that is more robust and easier to maintain over time.

Polymorphism in Dart is a powerful feature that allows for more flexible and reusable code by enabling functions or methods to operate on different types of data. By leveraging compile-time and runtime polymorphism, you can create code that is easier to maintain, extend, and understand.

12. Exception Handling in Dart

Exception handling is a crucial aspect of robust software development, allowing developers to anticipate and manage errors that occur during program execution. Dart, like many modern programming languages, provides a structured way to handle exceptions through the use of `try`, `catch`, `finally` blocks, and custom exception classes. This guide will explore how to handle exceptions in Dart, use `try-catch-finally` blocks, and create custom exceptions.

Handling Exceptions in Dart

Exceptions in Dart are objects that represent error conditions. They are typically thrown using the `throw` keyword and can be caught and handled using `try-catch-finally` blocks.

Dart provides several built-in exceptions like `FormatException`, `IOException`, and `StateError`, among others.

Using `try-catch-finally` Blocks in Dart

The `try-catch-finally` construct in Dart allows you to manage exceptions that may occur during the execution of a block of code. Here is a detailed breakdown of how to use these blocks:

`try` Block

The `try` block contains the code that might throw an exception. If an exception occurs, the control is transferred to the corresponding `catch` block.

```dart
void main() {
  try {
    int result = 10 ~/ 0; // This will throw an IntegerDivisionByZeroException
    print('Result: $result');
  } catch (e) {
    print('An error occurred: $e');
```

}
}
```

#### `catch` Block

The `catch` block handles the exception thrown by the `try` block. Dart allows you to catch specific types of exceptions or all exceptions using the `catch` clause.

```dart
void main() {
  try {
    int result = 10 ~/ 0; // This will throw an IntegerDivisionByZeroException
    print('Result: $result');
  } on IntegerDivisionByZeroException {
    print('Cannot divide by zero.');
  } catch (e) {
    print('An error occurred: $e');
  }
}
```

You can also catch the exception object and stack trace using the following syntax:
```

```dart
void main() {
  try {
    int result = 10 ~/ 0; // This will throw an IntegerDivisionByZeroException
    print('Result: $result');
  } catch (e, stackTrace) {
    print('An error occurred: $e');
    print('Stack trace: $stackTrace');
  }
}
```

`finally` Block

The `finally` block contains code that will always execute, regardless of whether an exception was thrown or not. This is useful for cleanup operations, such as closing files or releasing resources.

```dart
void main() {
  try {
    int result = 10 ~/ 0; // This will throw an IntegerDivisionByZeroException
```

```
    print('Result: $result');
  } catch (e) {
    print('An error occurred: $e');
  } finally {
    print('This code runs regardless of an exception.');
  }
}
```

Creating Custom Exceptions in Dart

In Dart, you can create your own custom exceptions by defining a class that implements the `Exception` interface. This is useful when you want to represent specific error conditions unique to your application.

Example: Custom Exception Class

```dart
class InsufficientFundsException implements Exception {
  String errorMessage() {
    return 'Insufficient funds in the account';
  }
}
```

```

You can then use this custom exception in your code as follows:

```dart
void withdraw(double amount) {
  double balance = 100.0;

  if (amount > balance) {
    throw InsufficientFundsException();
  }

  balance -= amount;
  print('Withdrawal successful. New balance: \$$${balance}');
}

void main() {
  try {
    withdraw(150.0);
  } catch (e) {
    if (e is InsufficientFundsException) {
      print(e.errorMessage());
    } else {
      print('An error occurred: $e');
    }
```
```

```
  }
}
```

Detailed Example: File Reading with Custom Exceptions

Here is a more detailed example that demonstrates how to handle exceptions when reading a file, using both built-in and custom exceptions.

Step 1: Define Custom Exception

```dart
class FileNotFoundException implements Exception {
  final String fileName;
  FileNotFoundException(this.fileName);

  @override
  String toString() => 'File not found: $fileName';
}
```

Step 2: Function to Read File

```dart
import 'dart:io';

void readFile(String fileName) {
  try {
    final file = File(fileName);
    if (!file.existsSync()) {
      throw FileNotFoundException(fileName);
    }
    String contents = file.readAsStringSync();
    print('File Contents: $contents');
  } on FileNotFoundException catch (e) {
    print(e);
  } on IOException catch (e) {
    print('An I/O error occurred: $e');
  } catch (e) {
    print('An unexpected error occurred: $e');
  } finally {
    print('Finished attempting to read file.');
  }
}

void main() {
  readFile('non_existent_file.txt');
}
```

Conclusion

Exception handling in Dart is a powerful feature that allows you to write robust and fault-tolerant code. By using `try-catch-finally` blocks, you can manage exceptions gracefully and ensure that your program can handle unexpected situations without crashing. Furthermore, creating custom exceptions enables you to represent specific error conditions unique to your application, providing more meaningful error handling and reporting.

In this guide, we covered the basics of exception handling in Dart, including the use of `try-catch-finally` blocks and the creation of custom exceptions. With these tools, you can write more reliable and maintainable Dart code.

13. Working with Collections in Dart

Dart provides powerful collection types to manage and manipulate groups of objects. The primary collections in Dart include lists, maps, sets, and iterators. This guide will cover each of these collections in detail with examples.

Utilizing Lists in Dart

Lists are ordered collections of objects. They can contain duplicates and allow access by index.

Creating and Initializing Lists

```dart
void main() {
  // Creating an empty list
  List<int> numbers = [];

  // Initializing a list with values
  List<String> fruits = ['Apple', 'Banana', 'Mango'];
```

```
  print(numbers); // Output: []
  print(fruits);  // Output: [Apple, Banana, Mango]
}
```

Adding Elements

```dart
void main() {
  List<int> numbers = [1, 2, 3];

  // Adding a single element
  numbers.add(4);

  // Adding multiple elements
  numbers.addAll([5, 6, 7]);

  print(numbers); // Output: [1, 2, 3, 4, 5, 6, 7]
}
```

Accessing and Modifying Elements

```dart
void main() {
  List<String> fruits = ['Apple', 'Banana',
```

'Mango'];

  // Accessing elements
  print(fruits[0]); // Output: Apple

  // Modifying elements
  fruits[1] = 'Orange';
  print(fruits); // Output: [Apple, Orange, Mango]
}
```

#### Iterating Over a List

```dart
void main() {
  List<String> fruits = ['Apple', 'Banana', 'Mango'];

  // Using a for loop
  for (int i = 0; i < fruits.length; i++) {
    print(fruits[i]);
  }

  // Using a for-in loop
  for (var fruit in fruits) {
    print(fruit);

```
  }

  // Using forEach method
  fruits.forEach((fruit) => print(fruit));
}
```

Utilizing Maps in Dart

Maps are collections of key-value pairs. Keys must be unique, but values can be duplicated.

Creating and Initializing Maps

```dart
void main() {
  // Creating an empty map
  Map<int, String> idToName = {};

  // Initializing a map with values
  Map<String, int> fruitCounts = {
    'Apple': 3,
    'Banana': 2,
    'Mango': 5,
  };

  print(idToName); // Output: {}
```

```
  print(fruitCounts); // Output: {Apple: 3, Banana: 2, Mango: 5}
}
```

Adding and Accessing Elements

```dart
void main() {
  Map<String, int> fruitCounts = {'Apple': 3, 'Banana': 2, 'Mango': 5};

  // Adding elements
  fruitCounts['Orange'] = 4;

  // Accessing elements
  print(fruitCounts['Apple']); // Output: 3

  // Checking for key existence
  if (fruitCounts.containsKey('Banana')) {
    print('Banana count: ${fruitCounts['Banana']}');
  }
}
```

Iterating Over a Map

```dart
void main() {
  Map<String, int> fruitCounts = {'Apple': 3, 'Banana': 2, 'Mango': 5};

  // Using forEach method
  fruitCounts.forEach((key, value) => print('Fruit: $key, Count: $value'));

  // Using for-in loop
  for (var key in fruitCounts.keys) {
    print('Fruit: $key, Count: ${fruitCounts[key]}');
  }
}
```

Utilizing Sets in Dart

Sets are collections of unique elements. They do not allow duplicates.

Creating and Initializing Sets

```dart
void main() {
```

```dart
  // Creating an empty set
  Set<int> numbers = {};

  // Initializing a set with values
  Set<String> fruits = {'Apple', 'Banana', 'Mango'};

  print(numbers); // Output: {}
  print(fruits); // Output: {Apple, Banana, Mango}
}
```

Adding and Accessing Elements

```dart
void main() {
  Set<String> fruits = {'Apple', 'Banana', 'Mango'};

  // Adding elements
  fruits.add('Orange');

  // Adding duplicate elements (will be ignored)
  fruits.add('Apple');
```

```
  print(fruits); // Output: {Apple, Banana, Mango, Orange}
}
```

Iterating Over a Set

```dart
void main() {
  Set<String> fruits = {'Apple', 'Banana', 'Mango'};

  // Using for-in loop
  for (var fruit in fruits) {
    print(fruit);
  }

  // Using forEach method
  fruits.forEach((fruit) => print(fruit));
}
```

Utilizing Iterators in Dart

Iterators provide a way to access elements of a collection sequentially without exposing the underlying structure.

Using Iterators with Lists

```dart
void main() {
  List<String> fruits = ['Apple', 'Banana', 'Mango'];
  Iterator<String> iterator = fruits.iterator;

  while (iterator.moveNext()) {
   print(iterator.current);
  }
}
```

Using Iterators with Sets

```dart
void main() {
  Set<String> fruits = {'Apple', 'Banana', 'Mango'};
  Iterator<String> iterator = fruits.iterator;

  while (iterator.moveNext()) {
   print(iterator.current);
  }
}
```

```

#### Using Iterators with Maps

For maps, you can iterate over the entries, keys, or values using iterators.

```dart
void main() {
  Map<String, int> fruitCounts = {'Apple': 3, 'Banana': 2, 'Mango': 5};

  // Iterating over entries
  Iterator<MapEntry<String, int>> entries = fruitCounts.entries.iterator;
  while (entries.moveNext()) {
    print('Fruit: ${entries.current.key}, Count: ${entries.current.value}');
  }

  // Iterating over keys
  Iterator<String> keys = fruitCounts.keys.iterator;
  while (keys.moveNext()) {
    print('Fruit: ${keys.current}');
  }

```
  // Iterating over values
  Iterator<int> values = fruitCounts.values.iterator;
  while (values.moveNext()) {
    print('Count: ${values.current}');
  }
}
```

Conclusion

Dart provides powerful and flexible collection types to manage and manipulate groups of objects effectively. By understanding and utilizing lists, maps, sets, and iterators, you can handle a wide range of data management tasks efficiently. This guide has covered the basic operations and usage patterns for these collections, providing a solid foundation for further exploration and application in your Dart programs.

Index

1. Introduction to Dart pg.4

2. Install Dart pg.28

3. Using an IDE for Dart with Examples pg.39

4. Basic Syntax of Dart: Variable Declaration with Examples pg.55

5. Operators in Dart with Examples pg.70

6. Control structures in Dart pg.94

7. Dart, functions pg.103

8. Object-oriented programming (OOP) in Dart pg,114

9. Create classes and objects pg.121

10. Classes pg.128

11. Polymorphism in Dart pg.132

13. Working with Collections in Dart pg.144

www.ingramcontent.com/pod-product-compliance
Lightning Source LLC
Chambersburg PA
CBHW071924210526
45479CB00002B/542